BOOKS BY JUDITH MARTIN

Common Courtesy: In Which Miss Manners
Solves the Problem That Baffled
Mr. Jefferson (1985)

Miss Manners' Guide to Rearing
Perfect Children (1984)

Gilbert (1982)

Miss Manners' Guide to
Excruciatingly Correct Behavior (1982)

The Name on the White House Floor (1972)

Common Courtesy

Common Courtesy

IN WHICH MISS MANNERS®
SOLVES
THE PROBLEM THAT BAFFLED
MR. JEFFERSON

by

JUDITH MARTIN

Atheneum
New York

1985

LIBRARY OF CONGRESS CATALOGING IN PUBLICATION DATA

Martin, Judith.
    Common courtesy.

        1.   Etiquette—Addresses, essays, lectures.
I.   Title.
BJ1853.M293   1985   395   85–47608
ISBN 0–689–11652–7

Published simultaneously in Canada by
Collier Macmillan Canada, Inc.

For a perfect gentleman

FROM THE

HARVARD COLLEGE CLASS OF '56

&

A perfect gentleman

FROM THE

HARVARD COLLEGE CLASS OF '88

*W*HEN I HAD THE
honor of giving Harvard University's John
M. Olin Distinguished Lecture, from which
this slender volume is derived, I became only
the second scholar from the rigorous discipline
of etiquette to address that otherwise distinguished center of learning.

The first was Cotton Mather, who many
times delivered himself of strong opinions on
the subject of Harvard deportment. He and
I have not always agreed about the fine points
of civility, but at least he was not given to saying, "Do whatever makes you feel comfort-

able," and "As long as you feel good about it, that's all that matters." The etiquette business is not for weaklings.

My celebrated predecessor's working method, developed in 1674 when he entered Harvard at the age of eleven, was to run to his father, who was then a Fellow and later President of the College, and report on classmates of whose behavior he disapproved. No one who has dedicated herself to the lonely task of perfecting American civilization, as I have, can fail to envy him this simple solution. If only I could snitch to Increase Mather!

It is not, however, my purpose to criticize behavior at Harvard. Indeed, I have encountered only perfect gentlemen with obliging manners since I first discovered the pleasure of paying social calls there, thirty years ago.

My mission, rather, is to call attention to the need for a philosophically acceptable and aesthetically pleasing standard of American etiquette. In my humble way, I only wish to finish the task at which our Founding Fathers failed.

My field work is somewhat different from that of other social scientists. Rather than examine a segment of the society for a limited period of time, or seek information through questions I have framed, I simply invite everyone in the country to write me at any time about any problem of the civilization. I highly recommend this technique, which brings me about two hundred letters a week, on a great variety of subjects. It also pays well.

I am indebted to those Gentle Readers throughout the world who generously contribute their observations and thoughts to the Miss Manners column; to Professor Harvey C. Mansfield, junior, who graciously invited me to lecture; to the Harvard University Department of Government and Institute of Politics and the John M. Olin Foundation; and to my editors who have become friends, and friends who have become my editors (in violation of the principles I state in this volume), including Wolf Von Eckardt, David Hendin, and Thomas A. Stewart.

It is my hope that this small treatise will cure the historic ills of American society. If not, it has at least already enabled me to endow, at Harvard, the Miss Manners Champagne Fund for Parched Political Philosophers, so that my successors at the lectern are immediately refreshed for their efforts.

Miss Manners has long held the belief that champagne is a major civilizing influence, not to mention an invaluable tool in softening up those who resist acknowledging the importance of etiquette as an academic discipline.

"But, darling, many very successful young revolutionaries—our own Thomas Jefferson among them—dressed for dinner."

Common Courtesy

In Which

Miss Manners

Addresses

the Question That Baffled

Mr. Jefferson

*I*N NOVEMBER, 1803, Thomas Jefferson, having achieved some notable successes in the field of restructuring society, dared to venture into the treacherous discipline of etiquette. His "all men are created equal" doctrine had obviously gone over in government, and he felt confident enough to attempt to apply it to manners.

The problem with which Mr. Jefferson wrestled, and which promptly defeated him, was how to adapt European systems of etiquette and protocol, based on court life and hereditary social classes, in order to make them appropriate for a democracy. It was a noble endeavor. From its birth, America has badly needed a way to express equality, individual freedom, social mobility, and the dignity of labor in the language of human social behavior (which is what etiquette is).

There was little precedent to go on. The abolition of *ancien régime* etiquette by French Revolutionaries was all very well, but who wants to watch a bunch of revolutionaries eating dinner?

Mr. Jefferson's proposed solution, only too vividly known as Pell Mell Etiquette, was to abolish entirely the concept of orderly precedence, as based on claims to social or professional rank. He acknowledged only distinctions of gender—now disappearing as a factor in etiquette—and between host and visitor.

Here is the complete text of the Memorandum on Rules of Etiquette that the then-President Jefferson sent to his cabinet:

1. *In order to bring the members of society together in the first instance, the custom of the country has established that residents shall pay the first visit to strangers, and, among strang-*

ers, first comers to later comers, foreign and domestic; the character of stranger ceasing after the first visits. To this rule there is a single exception. Foreign ministers, from the necessity of making themselves known, pay the first visit to the ministers of the nation, which is returned.

II. When brought together in society, all are perfectly equal, whether foreign or domestic, titled or untitled, in or out of office.

All other observances are but exemplifications of these two principles.

I. 1st. The families of foreign ministers, arriving at the seat of government, receive the first visit from those of the national ministers, as from all other residents.

2d. Members of the Legislature and of the Judiciary, independent of their offices, have a right as strangers to receive the first visit.

II. 1st. No title being admitted here, those of foreigners give no precedence.

2d. Differences of grade among diplomatic members, gives no precedence.

3d. At public ceremonies, to which the government invites the presence of foreign ministers and their families, a convenient seat or

*station will be provided for them, with any
other strangers invited and the families of the
national ministers, each taking place as they
arrive, and without any precedence.*

*4th. To maintain the principle of equality,
or of pêle mêle, and prevent the growth of
precedence out of courtesy, the members of the
Executive will practice at their own houses, and
recommend an adherence to the ancient usage
of the country, of gentlemen in mass giving
precedence to the ladies in mass, in passing
from one apartment where they are assembled
into another.*

As any Jeffersonian scholar will immediately recognize, this is the least edifying document that the great man bequeathed to his grateful nation. He might just as well have invented the protocol of the self-stick tag: "Hello! My name is TOM! What's yours?"

Under his system, everyone was frisked for signs of status at the White House door and stripped of all personal and professional rank. A foreign nobleman representing his undemocratic sovereign in an exalted position (probably having been conscripted for diplomatic service because he was disgracing his family at home, a personnel policy that used to make embassy social life so amusing) was treated exactly the same as the flunky assigned to clean up after him.

This novel democratic etiquette succeeded chiefly in giving everyone equal offense. President Jefferson was forced to modify it, and President and Mrs. Madison hastily wiped out any remaining traces.

IN THE QUEST FOR EQUALITY,
CIVILIZATION ITSELF IS
MALIGNED

*A*LTHOUGH HE
made such a mess with his foray into etiquette,
Mr. Jefferson—who, by the way, was as sus-
ceptible as the next Virginia gentleman to the
charm of polished French manners—was addressing what was, and remains, the great
American etiquette problem. Bless his heart,
he meant well. He was only trying to codify
his social ideals, which all good Americans
share. A number of our other distinguished
etiquetteers, such as George Washington, Ben-
jamin Franklin, Ralph Waldo Emerson, Har-

riet Beecher Stowe, and Eleanor Roosevelt, have struggled with this mighty task.

The state of American etiquette is, however, now worse than ever. Miss Manners is forced to act. I shall attempt to show what went wrong, and to proprose a modest solution.

In do-your-own-thing America, there is no longer much distinction between etiquette, the rules of behavior, and manners, the social premises from which they are derived. As the latter are constantly undergoing revision, one can get into serious trouble merely by following the simplest habits of one's youth. A gentleman who thoughtlessly defers to a lady can find himself labeled a pig; a young person taught to address elders in terms of respect may be scolded for making them feel old.

There is also an unfortunate tendency to confuse manners, which pertain to the outer person, with morals, which belong in such interior realms as the conscience and the soul. Religions generally put regulations about eating, dress, and washing in the same category as opportunities for sinning that promise considerably more fun. In Puritan America, acts forbidden by law included making nasty faces, jeering at others (or leering, depending on how attractive one found them), flirting, swearing, gossiping, and finger-sticking, a list practically constituting a catalogue of everything that makes life worth living.

I can understand the temptation of those who deal in both manners and morals, such as my colleague Cotton Mather and his friend God, to blur the distinction in order to be able to call out the moral militia for transgressions of manners. Threatening jail or hell is more effective and less wearing than the basic technique of those who merely teach manners, which is nagging.

However, the failure to distinguish between manners and morals also suggests, erroneously, that from personal virtue, acceptable social behavior will follow effortlessly. All you need is a good heart, and the rest will take care of itself. You don't ever have to write thank-you letters.

It is probably more sensible to hope that practicing proper behavior eventually encourages virtuous feeling; that if you have to write enough thank-you letters, you may actually come to feel a flicker of gratitude. "In truth," wrote Mr. Jefferson, "politeness is artificial good humor, it covers the natural want of it, and ends by rendering habitual a substitute nearly equivalent to the real virtue."

If not, good manners can at least put a decent cover over ugly feelings. Charming villains have always had a decided social advantage over well-meaning people who chew with their mouths open. "I could better eat with one who did not respect the truth or the laws," wrote Ralph Waldo Emerson, "than with a sloven and unpresentable person."

The belief that natural behavior is beautiful, and that civilization's restrictions spoil the essential goodness inherent in all of us noble savages, is, of course, the Jean Jacques Rousseau School of Etiquette. He began his career as a footman, and does not seem to have cared for it.

A major influence in Jefferson's time, Rousseau's philosophy continues to survive in the pop-psychology and "human potential" movements of today, and in the do-nothing school of child-rearing, which has given us so many little—savages. In point of fact, we are all born rude. No infant has ever appeared yet with the grace to understand how inconsiderate it is to disturb others in the middle of the night.

The concept that civilization is inherently corrupt, but Nature inevitably benign, is particularly popular in earthquake- and flood-ridden California. The natural approach to human relations presumes that to know any person well enough is to love him, and that, therefore, the only human problem is a communication problem. It refuses to admit the possibility that people might be separated by basic, deeply held, genuinely irreconcilable differences—philosophical, political, or religious. Thus, the effort to trivialize etiquette as being a barrier to the happy mingling of souls, actually trivializes intellectual, emotional, and spiritual convictions by characterizing any difference between one person's and another's as no more than a simple misunderstanding, easily solved by frank exchanges or orchestrated "encounters."

Many forms of etiquette are employed exactly to disguise those antipathies that arise from irreconcilable differences, in order to prevent mayhem. When I was president of a school board, a member with whom I disagreed on every possible educational issue suggested that we could resolve our differences if the trustees all went off on retreat and got to know one another better. "You don't understand," I had to tell him. "The only reason I haven't murdered you is that I really don't know you all that well, so I feel I have to give you the benefit of the doubt. Do you want to remove that doubt?" The reason that diplomacy is so stilted is that its purpose is to head off the most natural social relation between countries in economic or ideological conflict, namely war.

The charge is often made against etiquette that it is artificial. Yes, indeed, it is. Civilization is artificial. When people extoll the virtues of naturalness, honesty, informality, intimacy, and creativity—watch out. Honesty has come to mean the privilege of insulting you to your face without expecting redress, and creativity that it is wrong to interfere with a child who is destroying your possessions. It is apparently natural behavior to treat the sick, the disabled, and the bereaved with curiosity and distaste, but it is also highly uncivilized.

*T*HE IDEA THAT PEO-
ple can behave naturally, without resorting
to an artificial code tacitly agreed upon by
their society, is as silly as the idea that they
can communicate by a spoken language without commonly accepted semantic and gram-
matical rules. Like language, a code of manners can be used with more or with less skill,
for laudable or for evil purposes, to express a
great variety of ideas and emotions. In itself,
it carries no moral value, but ignorance in use
of this tool is not a sign of virtue. Inarticulate-
ness should not be mistaken for guilelessness.

Like language, manners pertain to a particular society at a particular time. If they were "just common sense," as is often claimed by critics of the field, why should Japanese behavior be any different from American, or medieval from modern? Like language, manners continually undergo slow changes and adaptations, but these changes have to be global, and not atomic. For if everyone improvises his own manners, no one will understand the meaning of anyone else's behavior, and the result will be social chaos and the end of civilization, or about what we have now. In a society that cannot agree on the simplest conventions, where people agonize daily about when to use first names and when surnames, whether to shake hands or to kiss cheeks, and whether "Have a good day" is a pleasant or offensive remark, it is little wonder that the citizens spend so much time shouting at one another in the streets.

Ordinarily, etiquette, like language, is learned by children imitating their elders, supplemented by an occasional parental plea that they listen to the rules rather than watch the action. The transmission from generation to generation occurs nonreflectively, so that the corpus of traditional etiquette is tacitly conserved.

But under certain conditions, people deliberately fool with the system, for philosophical or aesthetic reasons (classical Greece and the Renaissance were periods of great interest in etiquette), or to redefine, because of upheaval or uncertainty, who is in and who is out. The best way to play In and Out is to keep devising new rules of etiquette so that only the nimble can keep up, as was done at the court of Louis XIV.

Victorian manners were notoriously complicated for socioeconomic reasons. A threatened land-based aristocracy was trying to fight off the inevitable rise of newly rich industrialists, while the nouveaux riches were attempting to disassociate themselves from their former neighbors and friends. Innovations such as fish knives and forks allowed the rich to look down upon those who couldn't afford them; the declining upper classes fought back by condemning these implements precisely for being a parvenu invention. (Money is never mentioned in a properly fought social war; the polite way of saying you can't stand new people, still in use today for people who don't like the families into which their children are marrying, is "Those people simply don't know how to behave.")

The triumph of pragmatism that allowed the British aristocracy to survive is told in countless Victorian novels, where some young Lord Piffle falls in love with an heiress from what his parents consider a vulgar background. In extreme cases, she is even American. On due consideration of their inability to meet the castle bills, the elder couple pronounce the heroine sweet and pliable, and undertake to teach her the manners of her betters. With the understanding that the offensive, rich in-laws will visit as little as possible, the young couple lives happily ever after on his title and her money.

This is the sort of thing that gives etiquette a bad name. It is a wonderful instrument of class warfare, although that is only one of the many uses of etiquette. Those who conclude that manners are therefore merely an affectation of the rich to annoy the poor also overlook the fact that codes of manners are employed by all classes going in different directions. The most sophisticated and ruthless inventors of manners, with rigid regulations about dress, speech, and hierarchy, are teenaged street gangs.

In the upper reaches, the weapon of destruction always seems to be a fork. The earliest example I have come across was in 1005, when Saint Peter Damian treated the death of a young dogaressa of Venice as the opportunity for a most unpleasant ecclesiastical nyah-nyah. She had the plague, as did a great percentage of the population, but the saint attributed this young woman's death to God's retribution against her uppitiness, as demonstrated by the fact that she ate with a fork. She also took an occasional bath in fresh water. No wonder God struck her down.

The idea that good table manners indicate a lack of humility is still with us; to this day, a great many people brag about not knowing which fork to use. It is true that none of them catches the plague, but I have never quite understood how people can pretend that the fork is so difficult an instrument to master. If I could go from using a quill pen to a personal computer in three days, perhaps an ordinary person could, after seventeen years of in-house training, practicing three times a day, master the use of more than one fork. Perhaps not. The rationale that etiquette should be eschewed because it fosters inequality does not ring true in a society that openly admits to a feverish interest in the comparative status-conveying qualities of sneakers. Manners are available to all, for free.

The problem remains of inventing a philosophically appropriate American etiquette. It is easier to abolish manners than to devise new ones, but innocence and ignorance are not solutions. Well-meaning attempts of the last few decades again to eliminate distinctions among citizens of a democracy—this time also throwing out factors of gender and age—have failed because, like Mr. Jefferson's fiasco, they have been negative. Nobody believes that the man who says, "Look, lady, you wanted equality," to explain why he won't give up his seat to a pregnant woman carrying three grocery bags, a briefcase, and a toddler, is seized with the symbolism of idealism.

The Jeffersonian system of nonhierarchical

etiquette is, as a result of the neo-Rousseauism of the sixties, more widely practiced now generally in the society than he could have intended or imagined. The nearly universal use of first names nowadays, and other features of the model of instant-intimacy have all but erased such de facto distinctions as age, degree of education, professional rank, and increasingly, gender. Everybody is treated alike. This is the system, remember, that never did work.

What is more, the example is spreading, not only to our government, but to foreign countries, where forms of royalty and nobility are no longer as appropriate as they once were. Everywhere, politicians are experimenting with modern forms to demonstrate their ideologies. The ill-fitting double-breasted suit, for example, is thought to symbolize deep commitment to egalitarian precepts of Marxism-Leninism. (Our own leaders are given to explaining that they only force themselves to use limousine service, private office dining rooms, and such to save valuable time.)

The manners now coming into international use fit this intention even worse. When the rulers of the world go around hugging and kissing one another and calling each other "Ronnie" and "Maggie," they are not, to any student of protocol, using informality to express their identification with their own humblest citizens. They are harking back to the forms of reigning royalty, where kings and queens, more times related to one another than was good for their health, identified as a class. The correct form for kings and queens writing to each other, even if they are not of the same race, much less the same family, is *"Madame ma soeur,"* or *"Monsieur mon frère."* That concept of an international power club, with its own special bonds and loyalties, is elitism at its most severe.

One reason that the task of inventing manners is so difficult is that etiquette is folk custom, and people have emotional ties to the forms of their youth. That is why there is such hostility between generations in times of rapid change; their manners being different, each feels affronted by the other, taking even the most surface choices for challenges. Hair is always good for a family-splitting war. How it is worn is not the point—it did pony-tailed young men no good to point out the Founding Fathers' ribbon-tied wigs—because any style or length will do to defy another generation's style.

THOSE WHO WOULD CHANGE
THE COUNTRY'S MANNERS
ENCOUNTER CITIZEN RESISTANCE

*M*ANY PEOPLE RE-
sist any change in manners, no matter how
useful it may be. "Citizeness" never caught on
as a title in post-Revolutionary France, and it
seems that "duchess" never will go out of fash-
ion. In contemporary America, there is still
some bitter opposition to the title "Ms.," although it is in the best evolutionary tradition,
deriving, as did "Miss" and "Mrs.," from the
Elizabethan title "Mistress," which, before it
took on a racy meaning, had the same function
as "Ms." today. When the title was divided to
distinguish marital status ("Mrs." being used

properly only with the husband's names, and never the wife's given name), there ceased to be any correct way of addressing a married woman in a professional context. Such a person was not supposed to exist. Mistress Nell Quickly, the well-known businesswoman, had no such problem when she became Mistress Pistol.

At the same time, the very idea that life can be redesigned tends to create unreasonably high expectations—that we will finally get it right, and that existence will then be perfect. We Americans, as an optimistic nation, are prone to believe that new techniques are always turning up that will perfect life: that education can make people happy, patriotic, and ethical, not simply educated, as if that were not difficult enough; that art can be a deep, personal expression that is nevertheless universally accessible; that television and film executives could, if they were only willing, provide an around-the-clock choice of high quality entertainment; that therapeutic techniques exist which can remove all emotional pain; that a diet will be discovered that makes it possible to eat all we want and lose weight; that sex can be improved upon.

(I can't tell you how many people presume that I deal in a "new etiquette" that is required because of "the new sex." The new what? I know that it is widely believed that sex was invented in 1960 by two students from Berkeley—one of whom got a B-plus in life skills; the other being a graduate student whose degree was held up while the professors tried to duplicate the research—and that it only somewhat later caught on elsewhere. But I know that sex has been with us for some time, because it just so happens that I am actually a direct descendant, on both sides of my family, from people who practiced it. The only innovation of modern times seems to be discussing one's personal dissatisfactions with it at the dinner table.)

With this expectation comes intolerance for ambiguity, including those very polite fictions or conventions that smooth ordinary life. "Madam is not at home" was clearly understood, in the days of obligatory formal visiting, to mean, "Madam can't face you, any more than you can her, but takes due note of the fact that you have done your duty." Nowadays, we never allow ourselves the convenience of being temporarily unavailable, even to strangers. With telephone and beeper, people subject themselves to being instantly accessible to everyone at all times, and it is the person who refuses to be on call, rather than the importunate caller, who is considered rude.

I often receive mail from righteous correspondents who consider anything but blunt literalness to be dishonesty. They wax indignant because people who ask them "How do you do?" don't really want to hear about the malfunctioning of their bowels, and they demand an alternative to signing "yours truly" for writing those whose trulies they don't want to be. When smoking habits were considered a matter of etiquette, smokers (known then as "gentlemen") were easily kept from annoying nonsmokers (known as "ladies"). Now that it is treated as a moral problem, the smokers and nonsmokers are using not just smoke but emotional fire to kill one another.

In moral matters, duality is considered tricky at best, and so those who confuse manners and morals condemn the ability to use more than one set of manners. The person who refuses to dress appropriately for formal occasions "because my jeans are really me" achieves a sense of moral superiority from the simple act of offending social convention.

Those who believe in unwavering, literal truth also claim special license to be rude by giving unexpectedly truthful answers to such careless questions as "Do I look all right?" or "Would you marry me again if you had the chance?" I have always believed that the key to a happy marriage was the ability to say with a straight face, "Why, I don't know what you're worrying about. I thought you were very funny last night, and I'm sure everybody else did, too." Perhaps the greatest rudenesses of our time come not from the callousness of strangers, but from the solicitousness of intimates who believe that their frank criticisms are always welcome, and who feel free to "be themselves" with those they love, which turns out to mean being their worst selves, while saving their best behavior for strangers.

Finally, the trouble with inventing etiquette forms is that it is a game everybody can play.

Each person claims not only the right to design his own etiquette, but also to be insulted if others do not observe it, even if he has not troubled to acquaint them with his preferences.

Consider forms of address. In present-day America, there is no consensus on usage of honorifics and names. One man is insulted to be addressed by his first name, when it implies intimacy that he doesn't want; another is insulted to be addressed by title and surname because he thinks it makes him seem too old for intimacy. One woman complains that calling her Mrs. with her husband's name insults her by implying she is his property, another is insulted to be addressed any other way because she wants everyone to know how proud she is of being his wife. Listening to the rationale behind everyone's tiniest acts has added immeasurably to the boredom of modern life.

We have no agreement on what constitutes the basic social unit. It insults some married people to be invited only in tandem, because it shows a lack of respect for them as individuals, and it is even more likely to insult unmarried couples if they are not always invited together, because it shows a lack of respect for their "lifestyle." Some single people are insulted unless they are allowed to bring a date anywhere they are invited, and others if they are expected to do so.

It has never been easier to insult people inadvertently. A gentleman opens a door for a lady, because his mother taught him that ladies appreciate such courtesies, but this one turns around and spits in his eye because he has insulted her womanhood. A young lady offers her seat in a crowded bus to an elderly, frail gentleman, and he gives her a filthy look because she has insulted his manhood. Mind you, those are just people trying to be nice. The only problem is that they are operating on different systems of etiquette.

Curiously, it has never been harder to insult people intentionally. If you say, "You are horrid and I hate you," people reply, "Oh, you're feeling hostile; I'll wait until you feel better." Nonculpability, the idea that explaining motivation justifies any violation, is perhaps essential in a world of flying insults, where the all-purpose psychiatric excuse, "I'm depressed," is considered to absolve one of any obligation or responsibility.

The lack of agreement about manners results in an anger-ridden, chaotic society, where each trivial act is interpreted as a revelation of the moral philosophy of the individual actor, who is left standing there naked in his mores. We must standardize American manners, not only to complete Mr. Jefferson's unfortunately sidetracked project of developing a democratic etiquette, but to make order of the current chaos and to relieve people of the burden of developing and defending individual choices in the most common, everyday matters.

*W*HAT EXACTLY DO
we want? The ideals we had in mind, Mr.
Jefferson and I, are equality and individual
freedom and dignity of labor. I shall take the
liberty of adding equality for women, whose
interests, along with those of a few other people, he unaccountably overlooked.

I certainly agree with the Jeffersonian re-
jection of obsequiousness, and am frightfully
upset when snobbery makes a democratic people ape aristocratic forms. I had to grab for my
smelling salts when an American Chief of Protocol curtseyed to British royalty—we fought

a war over that point, and we won; why go back now?—and I have no patience with those who claim that they eat European style because "it's more efficient." If there is one thing our doctors agree on, it is that we should eat less efficiently, and as a matter of fact, the American style of switching the fork from left hand to right was the older European style that came here and stayed, while the fast-food approach developed over there.

I hope we can take it for granted that individual freedom must be tempered somewhat by the need for maintaining a harmonious society. I am not the only old crank who is being driven mad by the abrasiveness of modern America. When I am told nowadays of a "return to manners," and even credited with it, I am forced to reply that that is not quite accurate. People have indeed come to realize that they hate being treated rudely by others, but the solution they seek—amazingly, they apply to me for it—is the "put-down," a method of returning rudeness with even greater rudeness. It is surely a premise of democracy that the rules apply equally to everyone.

Equality is something we all agree belongs

in American behavior. But when we interpret it to mean a complete lack of recognizable distinctions among types of people, so as not to say classes, on any basis whatsoever, and a thorough leveling of all hierarchies, it doesn't work. What you have when everyone wears the same playclothes for all occasions, is addressed by nickname, expected to participate in Show and Tell, and bullied out of any desire for privacy, is not democracy; it is kindergarten.

Nobody believes in that kind of equality. Nobody really likes it. The de facto equality we have, of everyone's being treated at the lowest humanly possible standard of behavior, has not prevented tremendous striving to establish a recognizable class system. I am sorry to say that it seems to be a human instinct, once one has had the least advantage in life, to point out to as many people as possible that they haven't.

Unlike a hereditary class system, where titles fix the position of the upper classes, a fluid system requires blatant outward manifestations for renewed confirmation of status. The argument is often made that an institutionalized class system is, in a way, better, because people at least know where they belong and are relieved from constant competition. I notice, however, that this argument is always advanced by people who are satisfied that if a class system were newly declared, they would come out on top.

American class distinctions are made with money. Class distinctions everywhere have always been made with money, or its equivalent in land, and never mind what may have been said here or in any other society about blood or breeding or education or taste or nobility of character. That is an illusion. Fine feelings, whether intellectual, aesthetic, philanthropic, or spiritual, require at least temporary indifference to one's immediate financial gain. Generally, although not always, this means that one has already satisfied one's basic material wants.

Under a hereditary system, the dynastic founder who makes the money doesn't fully enjoy the spending of it. That is left for the next generation, the children who are brought up gently to acquire the refinement that comes to be considered nobility of character, or, put another way, who are spoiled rotten. In subsequent generations, the founder's money and their taste are used to accumulate possessions, and the patina of age becomes more highly valued than the shine of the new. In England, the traditional insult is, "They're the sort of people who buy their silver."

BANNED FROM TRADE, AMERICAN LADIES GO ABROAD TO ACQUIRE SUITABLE DRESSES AND GENTLEMEN

*I*N EUROPE, THERE WAS always that clear-cut division between those who made the money and those who enjoyed it. One was either in trade or one was in society, but it was impossible to be in both. (The item of men's clothing known in America as the "business suit" is, in England, called a "lounge suit.") The essence of being in trade is working to get ever ahead, while the essence of being in society is knowing how to enjoy the leisure afforded by having arrived.

Bridging this dichotomy diachronically, with earlier generations in trade and subsequent ones in society, is obviously not suitable in the land of the self-made man, where everyone is created equal. In nineteenth-century America, a synchronic solution was found, a sexually dimorphic division of the tasks of making and spending within concurrent generations of the same family. Until fairly recently, the pattern was that the father and sons worked, and, to whatever extent their earnings allowed, the mother and daughters were supposed to display culture, religion, luxury, and other assorted fine feelings of society (in addition to seeing that the housework got done).

This system of working men and supposedly leisured women is not as old as those who are trying to revive it, or to root out the remains of it, seem to imagine. Before the rise of the middle class during the industrial revolution, gender had little to do with whether one worked. All the poor, men, women, and children, worked, and all the rich didn't work. The nonworking of the rich was known as "looking after the property," a unisex form of housewifery, except that the man looked after the estate manager who looked after the outdoor property, and the woman looked after the household staff who looked after the indoor property. In America, rich men would satisfy our belief in the virtue of labor by venturing "downtown" to look after the cash property, but that was not supposed to interfere with leisure duties. Edith Wharton lamented the misfortune of serious male employment invading the upper classes at the turn of the century, and the demise of the long delightful drunken society luncheon. If only she had lived to see the coeducational expense-account lunch.

The American-style family division, by gender, of earning and spending made trouble from the beginning. When money made the women socially mobile, Mamma would take the daughters to Europe to find them noble husbands unsullied by work, and the last thing they needed to have around was old money-grubbing papa. Now even aristocratic societies are abandoning the idea of full-time leisure. There isn't a countess left in Europe who doesn't run a boutique, or aspire to, and every idiot son of an old family identifies himself as a photographer. We have also finally noticed that dividing the tasks of work and leisure by gender leaves a lot of dissatisfied people—overburdened men and bored women.

This system has now come to an end. We have tried to improve upon it by adding or subtracting, and ended up with twice-as-overworked women, and dropouts of both sexes from the professional structure, who couldn't figure out what to do with themselves and got zonked. College women are typically given to declaring for one or the other (in my day, for marriage; now, generally, for careers), and only later finding to their surprise that they must cope with both—while their men may be trying to figure out how to get out of doing both. The simple idea that everyone needs a reasonable amount of challenging work in his or her life, and also a personal life, complete with noncompetitive leisure, has never really taken hold.

ADMITTED TO TRADE, THE LADIES LEAVE THE PRIVATE REALM UNSTAFFED

A NEW SOCIAL PROB-
lem has replaced the old one. Now that vir-
tually everyone works, including middle-class
women and upper-class men, the private realm,
which included not only extensive family life
and society, but keeping neighborhood, civic,
philanthropic, cultural, and religious institu-
tions viable, has all but disappeared. There is
no one left to run it.

Everything is business. What is referred to
as society in the newspapers consists of parties
celebrating merchants or new merchandise, or
of charity luncheons or balls to which tickets

are sold. More exclusive, so-called private, social life is routinely used unabashedly as opportunities to further the guests' careers. The successful host is one who can command "movers and shakers," although it is not clear why one would want to have one's dinner table moving or shaking.

Such mongrel practices as expense-account entertaining, the tax-deductible home party, the private letter on office letterhead, the opening question at parties of "What do you do?" (still considered in Europe to be as rude as "How much money do you make?") are ubiquitous. In return for professional sponsorship of their entertainment, people have surrendered the very concept of leisure. I never thought I would see the return of cards, but everyone seems to have business cards nowadays to hand out at parties. Does anyone besides me still have social cards? Does anyone have a social identity?

Private houses are treated by their guests as public accommodations, or worse. A restaurant may be entitled to demand reservations, but a private invitation is not only not thought worth the bother of a reply, but considered an entitlement to bring along one's own guests. If the Second Coming were scheduled for next week, my mail would be full of letters asking, "Can I bring a date?" Even the White House has yielded to this, and issues "and guest" invitations. Mrs. Guest is the most popular person in the country—she goes simply everywhere.

Just about every etiquette question I receive concerning weddings provides financial information as the presumptive basis for my ruling on social matters. "We're paying for it ourselves, so why do we have to invite my mother's cousins whom I can't stand?" "If my stepfather is paying for the liquor, shouldn't he give me away, rather than my father, who's only paying for the flowers?" "How can we tell people that we already have all the household things we want but we like cash?" There seems to be a general belief that social, and even family, honors are for sale, and that there is an acknowledged admission charge to wedding guests.

Private standards, such as reticence and loyalty, have given way to commercial ones of advertising and competition. The best place to discuss your intimate problems is on television. If it is discovered that you are so successful that you don't seem to have any problems, it will be assumed that "dealing with success" is a problem, a chief manifestation of which must be the jealous resentment (politely called feelings of "inadequacy") of your family and friends. The friends you left behind professionally are as embarrassing in your new life as the relatives locked in the attic once were.

Business techniques are applied to the most personal situations. If you're ready to fall in love, you run a classified advertisement announcing a vacancy and including a job description with the most detailed skill requirements. It is permissible to fire lovers, but only with cause. "I don't love you any more" is not considered acceptable; "You don't meet my present needs" is more suitably businesslike. In what used to be known as free love, contractual obligation after obligation is being established until, ultimately, the free lovers will have reinvented marriage.

Friends are only friends if they fit exactly with one's stage of life and momentary interests. They should not only be able to advance one's career, but also to solve, or at least share, one's immediate social problems. That person whose agenda is to find romance doesn't bother with married people, and married couples only bother with people who are childless, if they are, or have children of the same age group they do, so that competitions can be held over which child first talks, gets into college, or marries. Acquiring or losing a spouse or a job means that one also loses one's friends.

I suppose one couldn't argue with applying M.B.A. techniques to running personal life if they worked. But loneliness has never been more widespread a societal phenomenon. There was no singles problem until singles got so single-minded that they stopped wasting time with anyone ineligible. Before that, it was understood that one of society's main tasks was matchmaking. People with lifelong friendships and ties to local nonprofessional organizations did not have to fear that isolation would accompany retirement, old age, or losing a spouse. Overburdened householders could count on the assistance not only of their own extended families, but of the American tradition of neighborliness.

NOW THAT SOCIETY IS
ABANDONED, ONE'S ONLY
FRIEND IS ONE'S BANK

*M*EANWHILE, THE empty forms of social behavior survive inappropriately in business situations. We all know that when a business sends its customers "friendly reminders," it really means business.

There is a pretense, by using the social model in commerce, that professional inequalities do not exist. "Hi, I'm Kimberly, and I'm going to be bringing you dinner. How ya doing?" "We're not just your bank, we're your friend." Never trust your luggage to an airline that has promised to be your friend, because the other side of that means that the business will not be held accountable any more than a friend would. Kimberly never does bring you the dinner you ordered when you wanted it, but is hurt if you complain. If a friend does his best, or has an excuse, or just botches something, or doesn't feel like it, it is rude to berate him for not doing a favor.

American businesses now seem to specialize in explaining to the customer why things were not done, rather than in doing them. "I wasn't here then," "We're short-staffed today," "That's not my responsibility" are the routine answers to complaints. Individual responses of nonaccountability are given, each employee refusing to accept the symbolic representation of the company. They are just there as "themselves," so the customer would have to be familiar with everyone's employment conditions and records if he is to find who is to blame for what has gone wrong, much less someone who feels interested in correcting it.

Using the social model, it seems rude to say, "I don't care how many people were out sick or whose fault it was—I want what I paid for." Of course the presumption that the customer is always right, or even that the business should be run for his convenience rather than the employees', is considered inappropriate among friends.

Privacy, or the ability to select one's friends on the mere grounds of personal preference, also comes to be considered rude. If everyone is a friend, one of them can't be excluded from the conversation just because he happens to be driving the taxi that the others have hired.

Nobody knows anymore what true social obligations are. A mockery has been made of traditional American openness, so that everyone is considered open, all the time, to all social advances. Where "the roof" was considered to constitute an introduction, the sky now serves the same purpose. In this age where people do not feel obliged to be polite to their spouses, I get dozens of letters from young ladies who want to know how to discourage the lewd advances of strangers without seeming rude. Sometimes they kindly specify that the method of fending off these men should not result in making them feel rejected.

This confusion of friendship and business not only blinds people to their own interests, but leads them to unrealistic expectations from others. I always have to start the New Year reading pitiful letters from those who, thinking the office Christmas party a social occasion where everyone is equal, used it to have a frank talk with the boss. I remember how handicapped my union, the Newspaper Guild, always was by the fact that reporters who called their editors by their first names and drank with them misunderstood their relationship at contract time. Much of the membership would act personally hurt and aggrieved by betrayed friendship—or else they would refuse to believe that their friends were acting in opposition to them.

One spring, I attended the Orioles' opening game of the baseball season in Baltimore—where the football team had just decamped to Indianapolis—in the company of Washingtonians who were still angry over the Senators' betrayal by moving away so many years ago. The perfidy of professional teams was bemoaned the whole bus ride to and from Baltimore. Fans are led to act on the personal model, which includes geographical loyalty, and so they are astonished and outraged when the teams, which are clearly in business, act, as they must, on financial considerations. It was like listening to a man who had married a prostitute complain about her infidelity.

IN WHICH IT IS LAMENTED THAT
LADIES ARE NOT TAUGHT THE
DIFFERENCE BETWEEN A
DRAWING ROOM AND A BOARD
ROOM

A MAJOR HANDI-
cap of women in the business world is that
while men were taught the difference between
social and professional manners—the phrases
"an officer and a gentleman," and "a gentleman and a scholar" suggest that different behavior is appropriate in the drawing room
than on the battlefield or even in the library—
women were brought up to have only one set
of manners. A woman was either a lady or she
wasn't, and we all know what the latter meant.
Not even momentary lapses were allowed;

there is no female equivalent of the boys-will-be-boys concept.

A lady (or a gentleman in the drawing room, for that matter) never discusses money, never brags, and never pushes or makes herself conspicuous. It is amazing, in this time of forgotten manners, how many women are reluctant to ask for raises or take credit for work done, attributing any career progress to luck. This does not make for great professional success.

Women are quite right to suspect that when social standards are applied to them at business—when the wrong person picks up the check at a business lunch, or a woman is accused of being "rude," rather than unprofessional, on the job; or supposedly insurmountable etiquette problems are cited as a reason for not giving a woman a good job—somebody is up to no good. At various times, the United States Government declared it impossible to find the form of address for the husband of an ambassador or for a female Supreme Court justice; and the etiquette problems involved if a woman were to become Vice President of the United States became a major topic of the 1984 campaign.

In the professional world, precedence is correctly based strictly on rank, not gender. If you are going to stand up for anyone, or get down on your knees, it is going to be for the president of the company, male or female; and the president always has precedence over the vice-president. It is as simple as that. The female equivalent of "Mr.," as in "Mr. President" or "Mr. Justice," is "Madam," as respectable a word as "mistress" used to be. (One wonders why professionally useful female titles always seem to pick up dirty connotations.) Spouses of officials have no official rank, but are accorded, by courtesy, those of their husbands or wives.

I don't in the least mean to suggest that I do not approve of an unashamed recognition of the importance of trade in American life, and of the dignity of all honest labor. But how can the equality of all citizens be represented symbolically in the decidedly unequal world of business, where some people are bosses and others are their employees? It cannot. Only in the private realm, where each citizen can exercise autonomy and choice, is full equality possible.

When there is no private realm, rank derives only from jobs, and a person without a job, no matter how charming, amusing, educated, beautiful, or rich, is a person without social identification or standing. This is why women who were once proud of single-handedly maintaining private, domestic, community, social, and cultural life for men who could manage only one job apiece, are now ashamed or defensive about being housewives. Many try to justify themselves by inventing pseudo-business titles for themselves, such as "domestic engineer," or reciting how much their skills would cost if they hired themselves out to their families. They are only conceding that it is more respectable for a lady to sell her services to her husband, than to give them away.

THE TRUE DEFINITION OF AMERICAN EQUALITY IS BEING TREATED "JUST AS GOOD AS ANYONE ELSE"

*T*HOSE CLEARLY LOW on the job scale—or even high but not satisfied with their positions—also harbor terrible resentment because they feel they do not have the equality they were promised as Americans. By equality, they mean not only equal opportunity, but being considered "just as good as anyone else" at whatever level they occupy. My correspondents always use that phrase when declaring their rights; I believe that is what American citizens understand to be meant by equality.

Of course, according to the American tradition, anyone who is dissatisfied ought to be able to work his or her way up. But even if this tradition accurately reflected the possibilities, the climb would rarely be quick or high enough, and if everyone did it, the ladder would topple. Nor is there any one rung that commands universal respect, unless it is that of celebrity, that super-category based on the lucky accident of having become conspicuous for whatever reason, good or bad. Perhaps that is because it skips over the old work ethic, which seems too slow and tedious now that everything depends on it. It isn't the climbing Horatio Alger whom we admire now, but the sitting Lana Turner, who is discovered at the drugstore counter and rewarded for simply being—whatever it is that she is.

The only identity one can still have as a person is as a personality, which seems to be something less than a person blown up to look like more. The ultimate advantage of this status is that the most trivial aspects of one's personal life, such as what brands of goods one uses or whether one has a quarrel with one's spouse, is marketable as advertising or "news," and the very experience of being marketable is considered excellent material for a book.

In that sense, fame equals money, but perhaps fame has actually replaced money. A "Do you know who I am?" system of precedence recognizes that famous people are entitled to special treatment (or, in a malfunctioning service society, to otherwise unavailable adequate treatment), which the mere anonymous paying customer, no matter how high a price he is willing to pay, cannot obtain. The celebrity is thus both a preferred customer, and a versatile and valuable item of merchandise.

When Americans believed that a job did not provide one's total identity, but was a temporary, voluntary, if necessary, situation, unrelated to a person's intrinsic worth and subject to drastic improvement in status because of the opportunities of democracy, it was not necessary to spend job time proving that one was not really what one seemed to be. An American in a service job—and our most prestigious job is that of public servant—derived his identity from his position in family, church, or community, and maintained his dignity on the job by remaining aloof from those he served. His friendship was not for sale. The etiquette writer Alexis de Tocqueville explained the impersonal demeanor of nineteenth-century American servants, unlike that of European lackeys and other menials, as an expression of the mutual recognition that "at any moment a servant may become a master. . . . Neither of them is by nature inferior to the other; they only become so for a time by agreement . . . beyond it they are two citizens—two men." One has to be an etiquette scholar indeed to remember that Americans did not accept tips until this century: We earned our wages and scorned condescending handouts. Whatever happened to that? one wonders as the dissatisfied taxi driver slams the door on one's fingers.

When there is no separate social identity, people are anxious to show on the job that they are better than their job rankings indicate. This is now done by one of two working styles: chumminess or surliness. These are two aspects—friendship and enmity—of the same inappropriate social model. Respectable women have always fought the idea that a pose of social availability be a requirement for jobs such as that of airline stewardess; now men and women inject a phony sociability, as opposed to impersonal pleasantness, into just about every service job. Botching the job is also considered a way of showing one is too good for it. But all the pseudo-friendship in the world, or the license for service people to insult those they serve doesn't disguise the fact that some jobs have lower prestige and lower pay than others.

THE TYRANNY OF THE
COMMERCIAL CLASSES

*C*onsumer competi-
tion is another, related, form of ranking, but
status-through-shopping makes inequalities
even more obvious. This is now carried out by
the very same people who make the money,
which may seem only fair, but this means that
the relative worth of the goods must be recognizable to people who haven't had sufficient
leisure to learn to make subtle judgments.
Clothes with the labels (designers' names) on
the outside, where everyone can read them,
are designed to meet this need.

In this competition, success is judged not by how old possessions are, but how newly acquired, demonstrating the ability to afford the latest designated symbol, even if that means buying up someone else's heirlooms. Not only humorists, but sociologists have been busy producing guides to explain what it means in terms of class to have wooden ducks in the drawing room, as opposed to industrial equipment in the kitchen. Personally, I see only two classes in America: those who believe in "making statements," as they call it, with dry goods, and those who don't feel they have to bother.

Curiously, this has come to mean that the rich, who were traditionally courted and served by the commercial classes, have now put themselves at the service of those very persons who have a financial interest in the competition for social standing. A lady has arrived socially when her hairdresser and dressmaker consent to grace her dinner table. Some of the credit for this clever inversion must go to the middlemen of modern art—the critics, dealers, and curators who, early in this century, managed to convince their patrons that by using their own money in the exercise of their own taste, they could make hopeless fools of themselves. That was the end of creative tension between artist or craftsman, and client. The days when an Isabella d'Este could inform a Titian what she wanted in the way of a nice picture are gone, although some not bad pictures came out of the exchange.

Now the principle of the incompetence of the rich regarding the spending of their own money has been extended from art to most other luxury purchases. A person who can afford it has an interior decorator to arrange his house, as he has a psychoanalyst to arrange his feelings. There is a professional expert for every aspect of life. No one who has enough money needs to worry about spending it in ways of which merchants might disapprove.

So the job of judging today's placements on the social scale has been turned over to middlemen who make money from it. Whenever you see a popular article about "making it," notice that the ultimate sign of success is invariably explained as recognition and approval from headwaiters. If the owner of a restaurant interrupts your dinner to greet you, life can hold no further glory. The expensive restaurant, with its mysterious allocations of good and bad tables, whatever that may mean, is apparently the temple of judgment, along with a place on Fifth Avenue called Trumpery Tower. Or something. Alas for my poor etiquette colleague Fanny Trollope, who invented the shopping mall, in Cincinnati, but failed because Americans of her day were apparently too sensible to spend their time running around some vast enclosed building buying things they didn't need.

DIFFERING WITH DIGNITY, A FOUNDATION STONE OF DEMOCRACY

*W*E NEED A COHER-
ent code of manners. I would prefer ratings
based not on commerce-dictated expenditure,
but on gentility of manners. We seem to be
gradually adopting a system of precedence
based on age, rather than gender, and I rather
think that is a good idea, as it gives everyone
a shot at being last and then first.

But please, let us not require people to pass
ideological tests every day. It is true that a society's manners must continually adapt to its
successively prevailing values, but etiquette
changes must, for aesthetic reasons as well as

the difficulty of disseminating them, be made at a slower and more graceful pace.

A standard set of manners also disguises the fact, inevitable and desirable in a democracy, that not everyone agrees on every issue. Unless we decide to make daily full public disclosure of creed mandatory (on T-shirts, tote bags, and bumper stickers), we should allow such issues to be debated voluntarily in political and other arenas, rather than inadvertently by those who are merely trying to go about the business of everyday life.

A RADICAL PROPOSAL TO PERMIT THE PURSUIT OF HAPPINESS

I BELIEVE THAT THE only hope for satisfying the American idea of equality of treatment in this society—being recognized as "being as good as anyone else" —is reestablishing the dualism of the commercial and the personal realms. By not separating trade and society in the lives of individuals, we force people to take total identity from their jobs, and therefore rob them of any realm in which human beings could and should have full equality in our society.

Instead of assigning people to one or the other by gender, we need to change the society so that everyone can enjoy some of each. The demands for these changes are implicit in the unhappiness of those unable to change the conditions of their lives, and in the increasing refusal to go along with them on the part of people in positions fortunate enough to design their own conditions.

The business realm must be structured to recognize that both men and women have personal lives. The modern professional world is still designed for an employee who is constantly available, because he does not have a family. He only has a wife who has a family. The pattern of the man always free for duty because he has a sham family and social life, which is actually entirely run by a woman, is disappearing; both men and women are less willing to settle for half a life.

Employers will have to recognize that employees—and not only women employees—have families, and therefore require certain scheduling adjustments to accommodate child-rearing and other personal duties and pleasures. For example, employers routinely allow for certain periods when employees will be absent—sick leave, vacation, military leave, and now maternity, and sometimes also paternity, leave—but there is no recognition of the need for time off when an employee's child is sick. Each parent has to find his or her own makeshift way of filling the gap between the end of the school day and the end of the work day.

The requirement of mobility for many careers is already becoming unfeasible. Couples who work require two satisfactory slots if they are to move, a fact that is recognized only when the employer is so anxious to hire half the couple that he somehow finds employment for the other half. Often, this results in the unfairness of a spouse's being given a job in preference to an otherwise more qualified person. Constant moving also means that one's only contacts are job-related, and effectively rules out community life.

Then there is that oxymoron, business entertaining. The chief purpose of business entertaining is to confuse people into applying social standards, such as loyalty regardless of merit, to business dealings. I don't think it works. It doesn't take much sophistication to figure out how to accept free drinks but still clear one's head for business. Having covered the diplomatic and White House official party scene during five administrations, I am cynical about the return that governments actually get for their kind tradition of providing certain employees with the approximate social style of nineteenth-century wealth.

The foreign service and corporate America are also finding that women are refusing to devote themselves, for free, to making those burdensome social schedules function. In some countries, the sole remaining task of royalty is to preside over the ceremonial part of government, for which they receive lifetime training and are handsomely rewarded. But America, while extolling the value of official entertaining, has never been willing to pay for professionals to run it, preferring to conscript wives, from the President's on down. In the bargain, it then villifies those wives for being social, and not serious.

Tax advantages for business entertaining, and deductions for memberships in clubs and other nominally recreational organizations, such as health or sports facilities, invite abuses of all sorts. It is commonplace for clubs to claim that their memberships are strictly social and their functions private, when legal requirements for nondiscrimination are in question, and that they are business associations for the purposes of tax exemptions. The individual freedom we value must include the right to bestow friendship as one chooses, but then why should government intrude into the social realm?

This realm, for which genuine time off from work is required, is for the pursuit of happiness. What constitutes any individual's idea of happiness, how it is to be pursued, and whether it will be found is not for Mr. Jefferson or me to say. Our idea is only to keep it free of ranking systems, so that all citizens are there accorded equal dignity. The restaurant table goes to the person who requested it first.

One should not be assigned one's identity in society by the job slot one happens to fill. If we truly believe in the dignity of labor, any task can be performed with equal pride because none can demean the basic dignity of a human being.

Off the job, there will be many attributes that may make one person more successful than

69

another, but these will be ones to which anyone can aspire, and which, in the absence of an objective ranking system, such as prevails in the business realm, different people will judge in different ways. I believe and hope that a revival of the private realm would preclude hierarchies in which absolute standards, such as job titles and money, rather than personal qualities, mark some individuals as obviously superior to others.

I think my colleague Thomas Jefferson would agree.

I'm not so sure about my colleague Cotton Mather.

Miss Manners is a perfect lady whose column is internationally syndicated by the United Feature Syndicate.

Judith Martin, however, also indulges in novel-writing, criticism, and even syndicated television. A graduate of Wellesley College, where she majored in Gracious Living, she is the author of Miss Manners' Guide to Excruciatingly Correct Behavior, Gilbert: A Comedy of Manners, Miss Manners' Guide to Rearing Perfect Children, The Name on the White House Floor, *and a forthcoming novel,* Style and Substance. *She lives with her husband and their two perfect children in Washington, D.C.*